"I have never known anyone to use t
with St. Paul, but then that good m.... ..a. never been more kindly
or cordially presented to us than he is here. Durepos, in his engage-
ment with Paul's writings, has discovered a winsome, yearning,
deeply attractive St. Paul. The result is a loveable book about a man
whom few of us ever think of as having been himself loveable."

—Phyllis Tickle, author of *The Divine Hours*

"Joseph Durepos's *A Still More Excellent Way* is both an invitation
and an invocation. An invitation because his moving reflections on
brief selections from St. Paul's writings entice us to read and medi-
tate on the saint's letters for ourselves. And an invocation because
the witness of his personal response to Paul's love for Jesus Christ
opens us to a cascade of graces."

—Bert Ghezzi, author of *Voices of the Saints*

"What a marvelous book! Every page is dripping with humanity
and spiritual insight. Read it. Share it. Allow Paul to show you 'a
still more excellent way' to celebrate and become the-best-version-
of-yourself!"

—Matthew Kelly, author of *The Rhythm of Life*

"Here is a simple but moving series of meditations on one of the
greatest of all Christian writers. Joe Durepos offers his deeply personal essays on St. Paul's letters, combining the author's insights on
books, history, food, movies, fables, family life, and work with the
fruits of his own study and prayer. Durepos shows how Paul can be
a gateway into a deeper relationship with God in our everyday lives;
and for that gift, we should, as Paul would say, rejoice!"

—James Martin, SJ, author of *My Life with the Saints*

"St. Paul needs rehabilitation in many peoples' minds and hearts, and this book is showing you a way to do just that! Knowing that Paul's letters were central in forming the Christian and even the Western mind, knowing you are going to continue to hear him on most Sundays of your life, knowing he could change that life in core ways, you deserve these inspiring reflections!"

—Fr. Richard Rohr, OFM, author of *Everything Belongs*

a still more excellent way

a still more excellent way

How St. Paul Points Us to Jesus

joseph durepos

LOYOLA PRESS.
A JESUIT MINISTRY
Chicago

LOYOLA PRESS.
A JESUIT MINISTRY

3441 N. Ashland Avenue
Chicago, Illinois 60657
(800) 621-1008
www.loyolapress.com

Cover design by Rick Franklin
Interior design by Joan Bledig

Library of Congress Cataloging-in-Publication Data
Durepos, Joseph, 1955-
 A still more excellent way : how Saint Paul points us to Jesus / Joseph Durepos.
   p. cm.
 ISBN-13: 978-0-8294-2758-5
 ISBN-10: 0-8294-2758-9
 1. Bible. N.T. Epistles of Paul—Meditations. I. Title.
 BS2651.D87 2008
 227'.06—dc22

                                                            2008014202

Printed in the United States of America
08 09 10 11 12 13 Versa 10 9 8 7 6 5 4 3 2

But strive for the greater gifts.

And I will show you a still more excellent way.

—1 Corinthians 12: 31

This book is for Betty, who has always shown me a more excellent way, and for Drew, Clare, and Lucy, among the greater gifts she's given me.
And for St. Paul, I will, *I promise . . .*

Contents

Introduction

This little book is the product of a year I spent reading, studying, and praying about the writings of St. Paul. I did a lot of other things during that year. I am a husband and the father of three children. I'm busy at my job. I have a long commute to work from my home in the Chicago suburbs. I also traveled, spent time with my friends, mowed the lawn in the summer and shoveled snow in the winter, fretted over the family budget, watched a lot of movies, and read many books. In short, I am a pretty ordinary guy. But, for this one year, Paul was my constant companion.

Why Paul?

First of all, I am fascinated by his story. Saul of Tarsus was a dedicated, committed Jew with a Greek education. He moved among the learned and powerful. He was a member of the Greco-Roman elite of the Mediterranean world. Then he met Jesus in a vision on the road to Damascus. Saul became Paul. His conversion was cataclysmic. It transformed him into an itinerant evangelist, a tent maker who wandered through the Middle East, Asia Minor, and Europe, telling the story of a crucified criminal whose kingdom, he claimed, reigned over all worldly powers. Paul's life captivated me. I wanted to know more about this man.

I also wanted to know more about his writing. Paul's letters are part of the founding documents of Christianity. All my life I have heard them read from the pulpit at Mass most Sundays. Yet much of the time they seem difficult, opaque. The syntax is complex, even garbled. Paul bounces around from the most elevated theological concepts to expressions of the warmest personal affection. I wanted to know more about these challenging, unusual texts.

But the strongest pull came from what Paul the man represents to me. Paul never met Jesus in the flesh. Yet he "saw" Jesus.

His relationship with Jesus was so vivid and so intimate that Paul counted himself as one of the apostles, the men who had shared Jesus' earthly life for years. I've never met Jesus in the flesh either. Yet I want to "see" Jesus. I want to have an intimate relationship with him. I identify with Paul. Or, more accurately, I *hope* to identify with Paul. Perhaps, I thought, Paul can show me the way to the relationship with Jesus that he had.

So I immersed myself in Paul. I read and reread his letters. I read books about him—scholarly commentaries, popular introductions, even a couple of novels, and I listened to audio CDs of his epistles. I watched several video miniseries that dramatized his life. This was hardly a systematic study of Paul. I fit it in with the many other responsibilities of a busy life. I did a lot of Pauline reading on the suburban Metra train and the Chicago "L" commuting to and from work.

As I read I began to see Paul's writing as an invitation that called for a response. Eventually I found the approach to Paul that worked best for me. I would reflect on passages from his letters, then I would write down my reactions. The habit of writing probably comes from my years of work as an agent and editor in the book publishing business. The habit of reflecting and responding is one that is highly prized in Ignatian spirituality, the spirituality that is most dear to me. I produced many reflections during my year with Paul. Here are fifty-two that I decided to publish.

These are *personal* reflections. That is, they are a reflection of me and my experience of Paul. Here you will see my attitudes, interests, and quirks. You'll see references to popular culture. I read best-selling books and I go to a lot of movies. Popular culture is where I live. It's where most people live (it's "popular" culture, after all). Some of these reflections are sad. Some have a touch of humor. Some are bemused. Some are fervent. All these traits are part of my personality, or so I'm told.

I am *not* a painstaking scholar by profession or temperament. I read many books about Paul and his times, and some of this background reading finds its way into these reflections. But here you won't find a lot of information about how and why these letters were written or about the religious and cultural setting of Paul's world. For example, I do not get into questions of authorship. I know that many scholars believe that some of the letters attributed to Paul were actually written by close associates who were influenced by his ministry. For my purposes here, I'm happy to accept the ancient tradition that Paul is the author of the letters attributed to him. Even if he didn't personally write all of them, they all reflect his mind and his heart.

Paul changed me. I hope he changes you. He can rearrange your priorities, cause you to think about things differently, and generate more patience, courage, and faithfulness in your life. He can show you how much you have to be thankful for. He can bring the purpose of your life into focus. Paul does all these things because he "saw" Jesus Christ. When he met Jesus, he met love itself. Paul was bathed in love, and this love took over his life.

I hope these reflections will be a gateway to Paul for you, and that the love of Christ will enter your life as well.

—Joseph Durepos

Examine yourselves to see whether you are living in the faith. Test yourselves. Do you not realize that Jesus Christ is in you?

—2 CORINTHIANS 13:5

Ashamed of the Gospel?

I am not ashamed of the gospel; it is the power of God for salvation to everyone who has faith . . . For in it the righteousness of God is revealed through faith for faith . . .

—ROMANS 1:16, 17

Do you ever feel uncomfortable about your faith? Maybe when in the company of people who are indifferent or hostile to your beliefs? Atheists have captured the zeitgeist, headlines scream with the latest sexual abuse scandals, and we read too many news stories about the damage caused by radical religious extremism. Ask yourself honestly: are you ever ashamed of being a believer?

In Paul's time, it was worse. Hostile Roman political power dominated the world. Greek thought was the prevailing intellectual currency of the day. The followers of Jesus were stigmatized because of their professed beliefs. In fact, it was dangerous to believe in Jesus during Paul's time.

We do face some of the same challenges the first Christians faced: how are we, as people of faith, to show up in this world we live in?

Paul says that our first task is quite simple—*do not be ashamed of our story*. To live as Christians, we must first find ourselves within the epic story of our faith. We must approach it with the awe and respect due a legacy of ancient and enduring spiritual heritage. We do this best by studying scripture, by prayer and instruction, and especially by learning the story of Jesus: his life and teachings, his death and resurrection.

When we embrace this great story, we open ourselves to a God who speaks directly to us and reveals our unique part in the unfolding story of salvation. This is God's gift to all who believe. This is what Paul was saying to the people of his time. I'm certain this is what Paul is saying to us today.

❤2❤

Paul's Astounding Conversion

I want you to know, brothers and sisters, that the gospel that was proclaimed by me is not of human origin; for I did not receive it from a human source, nor was I taught it, but I received it through a revelation of Jesus Christ.

—GALATIANS 1:11–12

Paul's conversion is possibly the most famous conversion story in the Western world. Paul never met the historical Jesus as the twelve apostles had. In fact he persecuted the early followers of Jesus. So what happened?

Paul claims that Jesus spoke to him and revealed his life's mission in one single, life-altering vision on the road to Damascus. He said he saw Jesus in all his ascended glory sitting at the right hand of the Father amidst the hosts of heaven. I think that Paul got a glimpse of the true nature of reality—a look behind the curtain—and chose to act because of what he saw, a vision of how life really is.

Paul immediately abandoned his former life and began praying, teaching, traveling, and sharing the story of Jesus as the awaited Messiah. The sworn enemy of the first Christian believers became the greatest evangelist of the early church. His life's work and writings were driven by the urgent desire that all people would come to know Christ.

Was Paul's ministry a success? It's been two thousand years now and there are more than two billion Christians on the planet. Not bad for a guy without a car, laptop, or cell phone.

⊲3⊳

Everything Created by God Is Good

Everything created by God is good, and nothing is to be rejected, provided it is received with thanksgiving; for it is sanctified by God's word and by prayer.

—1 TIMOTHY 4:4–5

Look at the world we live in. Consider what you see on television or read online or in the newspapers. Do you truly believe what Paul writes here—that everything God has created is good? Do you believe that "nothing should be rejected"? It's hard to believe this—at least on some days. Finally, how are we to be "sanctified by God's word and by prayer"?

I believe that Paul is telling us that the world and the people in it are inherently good because God created them. God wants us to enjoy what is in the world. However, there's one small caveat: we are to receive what life offers us with a spirit of gratitude, or as Paul writes, "thanksgiving." Gratitude becomes a form of prayer that invokes God's presence, and God's presence allows us to see the goodness in the world he created.

I see God as a generous but surprisingly reticent guest, waiting to be invited into the room, waiting to join the celebration, ready to share a wealth of gifts and blessings, ready to transform our world and give us a glimpse of the world to come.

I ask myself, What would my life feel like if I invited God in, if I began treating the world as holy, if I gave thanks for everybody and everything in it?

⫷4⫸

Everyone Who Calls on the Name of the Lord Shall Be Saved

For, "Everyone who calls on the name of the Lord shall be saved." But how are they to call on one in whom they have not believed? And how are they to believe in one of whom they have never heard? And how are they to hear without someone to proclaim him? And how are they to proclaim him unless they are sent?

—ROMANS 10:13–15

Paul is reminding us of our responsibility to share the good news. If we believers don't bring the good news to others, how will they know the good news? We are all called to be evangelists, according to Paul. We are all called to share the promise of salvation through Jesus. When we proclaim the good news, Jesus becomes present in our proclamation through the Holy Spirit. In doing this we create another doorway for God to work in the world—our world. This is the good news.

The question is: have I, have you, have we together, proclaimed the good news of the Lord today? "Everyone who calls on the name of the Lord shall be saved." With all the bad news in our world shouldn't I find a way to proclaim this good news?

Today, Lord, help me to share your good news by word, by action, by intention.

＜ 5 ＞

Love Never Ends

If I speak in the tongues of mortals and of angels, but do not have love, I am a noisy gong or a clanging cymbal. And if I have prophetic powers, and understand all mysteries and all knowledge, and if I have all faith, so as to remove mountains, but do not have love, I am nothing. If I give away all my possessions, and if I hand over my body so that I may boast, but do not have love, I gain nothing. Love is patient; love is kind; love is not envious or boastful or arrogant or rude. It does not insist on its own way; it is not irritable or resentful; it does not rejoice in wrongdoing, but rejoices in the truth. It bears all things, believes all things, hopes all things, endures all things. Love never ends. But as for prophecies, they will come to an end; as for tongues, they will cease; as for knowledge, it will come to an end. For we know only in part, and we prophesy only in part; but when the complete comes, the partial will come to an end.

—1 CORINTHIANS 13:1–10

Paul's eloquent words in 1 Corinthians 13 redefined love for the ages. This definition of Christian love has not been improved upon in two thousand years. But it's not simply the words Paul used that carried his message into eternity; it was his belief that gave them wings.

A church in a small village was celebrating its two hundredth anniversary and all the townspeople were invited. The special guest was an actor from the village who had gone on to become famous and successful. After dinner, the pastor introduced the actor and invited him to recite something. The actor stood, and to the surprise of many, began reciting the first part of 1 Corinthians 13—Paul's hymn to love. This happened to be the pastor's favorite passage of scripture.

When he was done, there was much enthusiastic applauding and cheering, and before he sat down, he turned to the pastor and invited him to recite 1 Corinthians 13 for everyone. The pastor reddened and said in a quiet voice, "I can't do justice to what you've just done. I'm only a simple pastor." The actor gently encouraged him to stand and recite the passage.

Nervous at first, the pastor began, *"If I speak in the tongues of mortals and of angels, but do not have love . . ."* As he spoke the familiar words, the pastor seemed to forget where he was and what he was doing. The room fell quiet and all who heard the pastor were moved to tears for they felt they were in the presence of the sacred. When he finished, there was a hushed silence in the room, and then thunderous applause. The actor put his arm around the pastor and turned to everyone and said, "You see, I know the lines, but your pastor knows the Lord."

✑6✑

The Measure of Faith

Do not be conformed to this world, but be transformed by the renewing of your minds, so that you may discern what is the will of God—what is good and acceptable and perfect. For by the grace given to me I say to everyone among you not to think of yourself more highly than you ought to think, but to think with sober judgment, each according to the measure of faith that God has assigned.

—ROMANS 12:2–3

The world has hierarchies of merit and status. Paul says that the hierarchy for those of us who are working to bring about the kingdom of God is based on the measure of our faith. Faith can be measured only by gentle and honest self-assessment—or "sober judgment" as Paul writes. The greater our faith, the greater our humility. We can rest certain in the knowledge that God gives each of us what is required for us to do what he's called us to do.

I was once invited to be interviewed live on national television to speak about the legacy of Pope John Paul II. The pope had just died and I was given about two hours notice before the interview. I had never done anything like this before. I had edited two collections of works based on John Paul II's writings but I was hardly an expert on his legacy. I'm an editor and layman who simply loved the pope. I was nervous. But it was an opportunity for me to share my faith by speaking about John Paul II. It was an opportunity that had to do with my faith, not my status or merit.

I did the interview, it went fine and I actually enjoyed myself. Since that experience I try to take Paul's words in this passage seriously. I try to be aware of what I am doing with the "measure of faith" God has given to me.

∝7∝

The Things
He Has Made

For what can be known about God is plain to them, because God has shown it to them. Ever since the creation of the world his eternal power and divine nature, invisible though they are, have been understood and seen through the things he has made.

—ROMANS 1:19–20

William Jennings Bryan (1860–1925) was a very popular speaker in his day, a three-time Democratic candidate for president, and a lawyer known for his confrontation with Clarence Darrow at the famed Scopes Trial. He was also a devout Christian and spoke openly and often about his faith.

Bryan once reflected on the watermelon seed and the process that turns one very small, black seed into a colorful, delicious, refreshing watermelon 200,000 times the size of the original seed it grows from. Not to mention that the watermelon is filled with dozens and dozens of seeds capable of growing even more watermelons.

In the Gospel of Matthew, Jesus offers one of his most famous short parables: *"The kingdom of heaven is like a mustard seed that someone took and sowed in his field; it is the smallest of all the seeds, but when it has grown it is the greatest of shrubs and becomes a tree, so that the birds of the air come and make nests in its branches."* (Matthew 13:31–32).

Paul tells us that the "eternal power and divine nature" of God is all around us. It's in the taste of a cold slice of watermelon on a warm summer's day; it's in the song of the bird in my neighbor's juniper tree. In order to "see" we just have to have a little faith, faith as small as a mustard—or a watermelon—seed.

∝8∝

All Things Created

May you be made strong with all the strength that comes from his glorious power, and may you be prepared to endure everything with patience, while joyfully giving thanks to the Father, who has enabled you to share in the inheritance of the saints in the light. He has rescued us from the power of darkness and transferred us into the kingdom of his beloved Son, in whom we have redemption, the forgiveness of sins. He is the image of the invisible God, the firstborn of all creation. . . . In him all things hold together.

—COLOSSIANS 1:11–15, 17

Paul was a charismatic, powerful speaker and storyteller. He possessed both an amazing ability to articulate spiritual truths and a deep understanding of the important cultural symbols of his time. Paul infused his teachings of Jesus with a currency and relevance that captivated his many listeners.

Let's join those listeners. Read the passage from Colossians on the left page silently and slowly. This passage is one of several hymns to Jesus that the early Christians sang. This is one of several that Paul included in his letters. Now read the passage out loud. Try to imagine yourself drifting back in time . . . maybe you're in a crowd of people, perhaps you're shopping in an ancient market square. People are gathering around a tent maker, hunched over his work, threading a needle. You walk over. He's speaking with a passion that captures your attention and the attention of the other shoppers and merchants. You press in closer, listening to this extraordinary teacher. He seems to be speaking to you—directly to your heart.

He is still speaking to us today, with words so eloquent and true that they've been echoing down through the ages for two thousand years. Just listen . . . *"May you be made strong with all the strength that comes from his glorious power, and may you be prepared to endure everything with patience, while joyfully giving thanks to the Father, who has enabled you to share in the inheritance of the saints in the light."*

≪9≫

Judge Not

You have no excuse, whoever you are, when you judge others; for in passing judgment on another you condemn yourself, because you, the judge, are doing the very same things.

—ROMANS 2:1

My wife has a friend who is considered a screw-up by most everyone. She drinks too much, has been in and out of prison a couple of times, and had a baby out of wedlock. But she's a wonderful person, my wife and I really love her. She's a good worker and a wonderfully giving person when she's sober. However, something inevitably happens that triggers a change in her and down she goes. Looking at it from the outside you might be tempted to judge her harshly. But there is something about her that most people don't know: when she was a little girl she witnessed her parents being shot during a botched home robbery.

In the Gospel of Matthew, Jesus says, *"Do not judge, so that you may not be judged. For with the judgment you make you will be judged, and the measure you give will be the measure you get."* (Matthew 7:1–2). Paul is echoing the very words of Jesus as he instructs the Roman community of believers to be careful how they judge.

This remains one of the greatest challenges to living a Christian life. As we move through our days, we must make decisions and judgments about what to do, how to respond to situations and people, how to process our feelings and tame our runaway thoughts. But Paul, like Jesus, is asking for something more. Paul is telling us to engage life with a spirit of generosity and charity and leave the serious judging of others to God and God alone. For the truth is, we have neither the wisdom nor the perspective to see and know what God sees and knows.

⤌ 10 ⤍

Be Courageous
and Strong

Keep alert, stand firm in your faith, be courageous, be strong.
Let all that you do be done in love.

—1 Corinthians 16:13–14

World War II was horrific. Millions died. Families were torn apart, entire towns were destroyed, and many countries still bear the scars sixty years later. I often wonder what I would have done if I were confronted by evil on such a grand scale.

Private Joseph Schultz was a marksman and a good German soldier. He was stationed in Yugoslavia after the German invasion of that country. One day his lieutenant called him over, along with seven other soldiers, and told them to march to the far side of the nearest hill where they would meet another officer who was waiting with their orders. As they came down the hill, Private Schultz saw five Yugoslav men and three women huddled together and under guard. The young officer ordered the eight soldiers to form a line and prepare to execute the prisoners. He shouted, "Ready," then "Aim." Suddenly Private Schultz threw down his rifle and helmet and walked toward the men and women waiting to be executed. The officer ordered him to stop and to return to the firing squad. Private Schultz took his place in the middle of the Yugoslavians and reached out and grabbed the hands of the man and woman standing on either side of him. The officer angrily yelled, "Fire."

Private Schultz died that day, his blood spilled and mingling with those he was there to kill. Among the things found on his body was a scrap of paper with these handwritten words from Paul, "Love does not delight in evil, but rejoices in the truth. Love always protects, always trusts, always hopes and always perseveres."

What's the Price
of Contentment?

There is great gain in godliness combined with contentment; for
we brought nothing into the world, so that we can take nothing
out of it; but if we have food and clothing, we will be content
with these. But those who want to be rich fall into temptation
and are trapped by many senseless and harmful desires that
plunge people into ruin and destruction. For the love of money
is a root of all kinds of evil, and in their eagerness to be rich
some have wandered away from the faith and pierced themselves
with many pains.

—1 TIMOTHY 6:6–10

The love of money is the root of all evil. How many times have you heard this? Do you believe it? Living in the United States, I see little evidence that people really believe it. Many of us are literally working ourselves to death—where's the "contentment," the "godliness" in that? Of course, we remind ourselves that it's not actually the money that's the root of all evil; it's the *love* of money that's the problem. We don't love it; we just need more and more of it. What would it take to really be content with what we already have? I don't know . . .

There was a very poor young boy who discovered a pearl of great wealth. He realized at once that if he sold this pearl he and his family would have all the money they might need. But when he tried to sell the pearl, the buyers proved devious and tried to trick the boy into selling the pearl for far less than it was worth. When that didn't work they resorted to hiring thugs to attack him and his family and steal the pearl. Once the boy understood what was happening, he went to the beach and in plain sight of everyone—including the pearl merchants—threw the pearl as far out into the ocean as he could and his life returned to normal, still poor, but content.

∝12∝

The Interests
of Others

If then there is any encouragement in Christ, any consolation from love, any sharing in the Spirit, any compassion and sympathy, make my joy complete: be of the same mind, having the same love, being in full accord and of one mind. Do nothing from selfish ambition or conceit, but in humility regard others as better than yourselves. Let each of you look not to your own interests, but to the interests of others.

—PHILIPPIANS 2:1–4

Paul preached a radically countercultural message. He taught exactly what Jesus taught in the Beatitudes: care for the weak and the poor. This was precisely contrary to values of the ancient Greek and Roman world. Influential Romans and Greeks of Paul's time placed much value on individual strength and self-sufficiency. The strong were revered and the weak were often cast aside. In much of the ancient world, the poor and the handicapped were thought to be cursed or punished by the gods.

Paul preached exactly the opposite. He traveled around with this simple message: be of humble spirit, reach out and take care of those in need, act with compassion toward all people and in all situations, have sympathy for those in distress. He said that in caring for the most marginalized we will find our salvation. This message was a tough sell. It wasn't easy when Jesus first preached it; it wasn't any easier when Paul and the first disciples spread the word.

Today, largely because of the Gospel, an awareness of the poor and the infirm is part of our Christian worldview. But many of us live comfortable lives and seldom have contact with the least fortunate among us. Paul is asking us for more than an attitude change, he's asking us to change our actions, our behavior, and to consciously seek out those who desperately need our help. Our faith as Christians propels us forward to bring the consolation of love we experience through Christ to the world where it's needed most.

⪥13⪤

The Body of Christ

The gifts he gave were that some would be apostles, some prophets, some evangelists, some pastors and teachers, to equip the saints for the work of ministry, for building up the body of Christ, until all of us come to the unity of the faith and of the knowledge of the Son of God, to maturity, to the measure of the full stature of Christ. We must no longer be children, tossed to and fro and blown about by every wind of doctrine, by people's trickery, by their craftiness in deceitful scheming. But speaking the truth in love, we must grow up in every way into him who is the head, into Christ, from whom the whole body, joined and knit together by every ligament with which it is equipped, as each part is working properly, promotes the body's growth in building itself up in love.

—EPHESIANS 4:11–16

When I was in high school, Harry Chapin had a huge hit with the song, "Cat's in the Cradle." It tells the story of a father who doesn't grow up in time to give his son the attention he needs. Indifference to his family is the legacy he passes on to his son. I remember praying before I was married, before I had a son of my own, Lord please help me to grow up and be there for my child. Don't let me squander the time I've been given.

In this passage, Paul is exhorting us to grow up, become adults, and be grounded in Christ: "we must no longer be children, tossed to and fro." Each of us is given certain "gifts" and with these gifts we each contribute to the building of the authentic church on earth—the body of Christ. Doing this requires a certain maturity: *"we must grow up in every way into him who is the head, into Christ."* For Paul, this is not a mysterious task. It's part of the natural course of life as we grow as Christians. We need to have hope in God and a willingness to step up and take our part in building the kingdom.

We're all called to grow in maturity through the Holy Spirit. Ask yourself: Am I growing up in my faith? Am I saying yes to God as an adult? Am I taking responsibility for using the "gifts" I've been given by God?

⊂14⊃

God's Kindness

*Do you not realize that God's kindness is meant
to lead you to repentance?*

—ROMANS 2:4

To repent means to change course—to turn away from sin and embrace the good. When we repent we express sorrow about what we've done and ask forgiveness from God. And here's the miracle: God always receives us back.

God's tenderness is a gentle invitation to renounce a troublesome activity or destructive behavior. I see it as a chance for me to rethink my painful thoughts and unwholesome attitudes. But God's love is a wonder. What does it mean to be in relationship with a God who gently but persistently welcomes me back every time I turn away? Why should God in all his glory care about my relationship with him?

The Jesuit writer Father William Barry gave me a startling insight into these questions: God craves our friendship. He wants to be our friend, not out of need or loneliness, but out of unconditional and abundant love for us personally. God wants me to love him as much as he loves me. That's a staggering thought: God wants to be in a relationship with me as a friend. What does this love feel like?

There was a little girl who was born with a facial deformity and deafness in one ear. She was teased relentlessly by her classmates, as are many such children. She couldn't hide her face, but worked hard to disguise her deafness. She passed the annual hearing test at school by not covering her good ear completely with her hand when her bad ear was tested. She could hear just enough with her good ear what was being said by the person giving her the test. One year, her favorite teacher gave the test, a woman who had always treated her with respect and loving kindness. When it came time to test her bad ear, she held her hand close and waited for the whispered words. The teacher spoke seven words that she never forgot: "I wish you were my little girl."

❧ 15 ❧

You Know What Time It Is

Love does no wrong to a neighbor; therefore, love is the fulfilling of the law. Besides this, you know what time it is, how it is now the moment for you to wake from sleep. For salvation is nearer to us now than when we became believers; the night is far gone, the day is near. Let us then lay aside the works of darkness and put on the armor of light.

—Romans 13:10–12

*Y*ou *know what time it is."* Paul is writing in his most urgent mode. *Love does no wrong to a neighbor.* In the ancient tradition of the Torah, a neighbor was considered kin, but in the emerging Jesus tradition *neighbor* expanded to include all the people in our community. The "time" Paul is writing about is *kairos*, a Greek word meaning a critical time when something important is about to occur. For Paul, Jesus' coming heralded the dawning of a new world, a spiritual age of love, the fulfillment of all prophecy. One world was fading, another was emerging. But meanwhile, as the new world was being born, there was still danger and believers needed to remain vigilant.

For several years now, between Christmas Day and New Year's Day, my wife and I watch Peter Jackson's *The Lord of the Rings* movies—all three, extended DVD versions. I love the whole saga, but my favorite is the first film, *The Fellowship of the Ring.* I especially love the scene in the mines of Moria, when Frodo and Gandalf are talking about the ring of power. Frodo is having second thoughts about what the ring has brought into his life and into the world. He says to Gandalf, "I wish none of this had happened." Gandalf responds, "So do all who live to see such times. But that is not for them to decide. All we have to decide is what to do with the time that is given to us."

I see Gandalf as Paul—sometimes fierce, maybe even a little dangerous, but bridging the worlds of what is and what's to come, helping us to see the consequences of the choices that we make. Paul didn't see God working retail—simply saving one soul at a time. God was working wholesale—he had a cosmic plan for salvation, a plan that was moving forward with incredible speed to embrace everyone and everything. For Paul, the stakes were as high as they can be: an age of love and light was dawning and everyone needed to play their parts to make sure it happened.

✠ 16 ✠

All Shall Be Well

I want you to be free from anxieties.

—1 Corinthians 7:32

I love this line from Paul's letter to the Corinthians. It's buried in a passage where he's speaking about marriage, being single, and other relationship issues. Sometimes, when I read this passage I can imagine Paul preaching to a large audience and then pausing and turning toward me and saying, "I want you to be free from anxieties—*you* Joe, I want *you* to be free from anxieties."

What's interesting is that Paul believed Christians were already living an existence more defined by the coming heavenly reality than their present earthly existence. Since in heaven there will be no worries, no problems, Paul was gently suggesting to his readers that part of our life in Christ is to live free of our anxieties here and now. To understand that through Christ we can know heaven on earth.

Dame Julian of Norwich said it famously when she wrote, "All shall be well, and all shall be well, and all manner of thing shall be well." This seems to be a lesson all the great saints knew. But one I need to hear over and over again.

❧17❧

We Are the Lord's

We do not live to ourselves, and we do not die to ourselves. If we live, we live to the Lord, and if we die, we die to the Lord; so then, whether we live or whether we die, we are the Lord's. For to this end Christ died and lived again, so that he might be Lord of both the dead and the living.

—ROMANS 14:7–9

Paul was not afraid to die, not because he was cavalier about life, but because Jesus conquered death through his sacrifice on the cross. Paul believed all existence was governed by God's will, including life and death, and for those who believe in Christ there is no real death but rather the promise of eternal life.

Ask yourself honestly: Paul believed this; do you? Paul is making some pretty unequivocal claims. I want to believe it, I really do, but the only way I can believe is by embracing this thing called faith. I need to believe without proof. But doesn't my heart tell me that God is active in my life and the lives of those around me? Don't I have the Gospels, the witness of the saints, and the teachings of the church? Haven't I experienced the grace, mercy, and love of God many times? How much proof do I need?

Martin Luther wrote this in his famous preface to Paul's letter to the Romans: "Faith is a living, unshakeable confidence in God's grace; it is so certain, that someone would die a thousand times for it. This kind of trust in and knowledge of God's grace makes a person joyful, confident, and happy with regard to God and all creatures. This is what the Holy Spirit does by faith."

✙18✙

The Foremost Sinner

I am grateful to Christ Jesus our Lord, who has strengthened me, because he judged me faithful and appointed me to his service, even though I was formerly a blasphemer, a persecutor, and a man of violence. But I received mercy because I had acted ignorantly in unbelief, and the grace of our Lord overflowed for me with the faith and love that are in Christ Jesus.

The saying is sure and worthy of full acceptance, that Christ Jesus came into the world to save sinners—of whom I am the foremost. But for that very reason I received mercy, so that in me, as the foremost, Jesus Christ might display the utmost patience, making me an example to those who would come to believe in him for eternal life. To the King of the ages, immortal, invisible, the only God, be honor and glory forever and ever. Amen.

—1 TIMOTHY 1:12–17

None of us are perfect and certainly Paul never claimed to be perfect. In fact, numerous times he establishes his credentials by pointing out how sinful he was and how merciful God is. Christ Jesus came into the world to save sinners—and Paul identifies himself as the foremost sinner.

There is a priest I admire a great deal, who lives and works with homeless men in Chicago. He is known and admired widely for this particular ministry though he's very humble about what he does. One day we were having lunch and I asked him about a personal matter to get his advice. He gently declined to offer his perspective by saying, "I wouldn't know, Joe, I am such a big sinner myself I wouldn't even try to tell you what to do regarding this." I looked at him, searching for the irony in his answer, and saw instead he was entirely serious. Rather than being upset for not getting the answer I was seeking, I found it surprisingly freeing to be with such an honest and good man.

See, the thing is, we're all sinners, we're all struggling, and we're all counting on God's mercy. If I'm putting off doing good in the world until I have my leadership license, my master's degree in moral certitude, or until the world recognizes how much I've grown spiritually—well, that day may never come. I need to listen to what Paul is saying and make myself available to the Lord and trust that he'll do the rest when the time is right.

⽈19⽇

Light to Things Now Hidden in Darkness

Do not pronounce judgment before the time, before the Lord comes, who will bring to light the things now hidden in darkness and will disclose the purposes of the heart.

—1 Corinthians 4:5

I worry sometimes about things I've done and things I should have done. In my darker moments I feel myself shielding these things away from the Lord, imagining somehow I can hide these things from God. Why? Is it shame? Fear? I can't even explain to myself why I think, do, and say certain things. I need the Lord's help. I welcome the Lord's scrutiny; I know that his judgment comes with mercy and healing. I'm tired; I don't want to have any more secrets or holdbacks from the Lord.

There was a cave deep in the Earth that had never seen light. One day the sun invited the cave to come up and visit. The cave did, and it was dazzled by the light of the sun. The cave found the sun's warmth so comforting that it was overcome by gratitude. In return, the cave invited the sun to come for a visit because the sun had never seen darkness before. When the day came, the sun descended to the cave, excited and eager to see the darkness. As the sun entered the cave it became puzzled and asked the cave, "Where is the darkness?"

When the Lord comes it's possible the things we've kept hidden in the dark will no longer be visible and all that we'll be left holding is the courage we've shown by inviting the Lord into our lives, finally.

⨯20⨯

Devote Yourselves to Prayer

Devote yourselves to prayer,
keeping alert in it with thanksgiving.

—Colossians 4:2

Paul writes about prayer constantly in his letters, and he undoubtedly spent a lot of time praying. For Paul the life in Christ begins with prayer. Prayer means making the mind attentive to God; prayer includes gratitude for what's been given. This passage is like Paul's mantra: pray always, pay attention, be grateful. This is crucial to understanding how Paul proceeded in the world.

Ignatius of Loyola was greatly inspired by Paul. He is credited with having written "Pray as if everything depended on God. Work as if everything depended on you." The Ignatian form of spirituality that I follow involves a mindfulness that calls me to always be aware of where God is in my life. I do this by seeking God in the moments and activities of my days and nights, by reflecting on how I've experienced God, and learning from my experience and moving forward with the trust and understanding that comes from being in relationship with God. It is a way of proceeding that serves a plodder like me.

I believe all of us can find great strength in walking the path that Paul and Ignatius have set before us. It's often said that others can tell a lot about us by the company we keep. In prayer, we begin to close the gap between the greatest of these saints and ourselves, we enter their company, and we're blessed to be among them.

ᕦ21ᕤ

As for You, Young Man of God

As for you, man of God . . . pursue righteousness, godliness, faith, love, endurance, gentleness. Fight the good fight of the faith . . . I charge you to keep the commandment without spot or blame until the manifestation of our Lord Jesus Christ, which he will bring about at the right time—he who is the blessed and only Sovereign, the King of kings and Lord of lords. It is he alone who has immortality and dwells in unapproachable light, whom no one has ever seen or can see; to him be honor and eternal dominion. Amen.

—1 TIMOTHY 6:11–12, 13–16

It feels as if Paul is commissioning us in the King's service with this reading, calling us to serve the Lord, the one who "dwells in unapproachable light." How we honor that call is the life challenge each of us must rise to.

There was a beloved king who had two sons. He was growing older and the time was approaching for him to choose one of his sons to become the next king. After consulting with his council of elders, he called the two men to his hall. He gave each of them six silver pieces and explained that their task was to fill the giant hall before the moon was at its highest that very day. Whichever one could do it most completely, would be the new king.

The older son went out into his father's fields where the hay was being harvested. He gave the foreman the six silver pieces and the foreman had his men move all the hay into the hall. The hay nearly filled the hall to the high ceilings. The older brother demanded that his father make him the new king. The king said, "The moon is not yet high in the heavens, your brother still has time, let's see what happens."

When it was dark, the younger brother returned to the hall. He asked that all the lights be dimmed and the hay be removed from the hall. Just as the moon climbed to its highest point in the sky, the younger brother lit a small candle in the darkened hall. Slowly, the glow of the candle filled the entire room and the younger brother walked to up to his father and handed him back the six silver pieces.

The king smiled at his son and said, "You will be my heir. Your brother filled my hall with hay. You have filled my hall with light, the very thing my people need."

22

The Spirit of God

No one comprehends what is truly God's except the Spirit of God. Now we have received not the spirit of the world, but the Spirit that is from God, so that we may understand the gifts bestowed on us by God. And we speak of these things in words not taught by human wisdom but taught by the Spirit, interpreting spiritual things to those who are spiritual.

—I Corinthians 2:11–13

All of us know more than one language. Some learn Spanish or French or another language in school, but there are other languages that we learn. Our families will often have a unique way of communicating with words and gestures. At work we learn the special words and actions unique to our profession. We survive in the world by conveying what needs to be said or shown in a manner that will be understood by those we're communicating with.

God also has a language. This is what Paul is speaking about. The Holy Spirit speaks to us of the gifts, the graces, the wisdom of God. The Holy Spirit is God's radio signal. We need to turn on and tune in if we want to experience what God is offering us. We can do this through silence, through listening deeply to other people, through prayer and worship, through reading and music, through just noticing what's going on around us.

Unfortunately, there's a lot of static out there. Sometimes the signal can be hard to pick up. God is communicating but we're not tuned in. The Holy Spirit is the free, high quality broadcasting source of God's inspiration beaming a signal every minute of every day right into our minds and hearts. How's your reception?

❧23❧

Working Out
Our Salvation

Therefore, my beloved, just as you have always obeyed me, not only in my presence, but much more now in my absence, work out your own salvation with fear and trembling; for it is God who is at work in you, enabling you both to will and to work for his good pleasure. Do all things without murmuring and arguing, so that you may be blameless and innocent, children of God without blemish in the midst of a crooked and perverse generation, in which you shine like stars in the world.

—PHILIPPIANS 2:12–15

I'm married and the father of three children. I confess I worry about everything: money, jobs, the health of my wife and children, whether my children will finish school, whether they'll find suitable careers, settle down with someone they love and who loves them. The list goes on and on.

I take great comfort in the way of Paul. Paul is writing this letter from a jail cell; scholars are not sure where. The news from Philippi, one of his favorite communities, is bad. The Philippians are experiencing problems within their community and hostility from outside it. They are in a fragile state and if they aren't careful things could get worse, even dangerous.

In spite of being in jail, in spite of the possibility of execution, read how gentle and reassuring Paul is with his friends in Philippi: *"my beloved,"* God is *"at work in you,"* *"be blameless and innocent, children of God,"* *"you shine like the stars."* As a Christian in the twenty-first century we can learn much from Paul about being encouraging and loving in the real world.

∝24∝

When I Was a Child

When I was a child, I spoke like a child, I thought like a child, I reasoned like a child; when I became an adult, I put an end to childish ways. For now we see in a mirror, dimly, but then we will see face to face. Now I know only in part; then I will know fully, even as I have been fully known. And now faith, hope, and love abide, these three; and the greatest of these is love.

—1 CORINTHIANS 13:11–13

This reading from 1 Corinthians is one of the most famous passages from Scripture, in fact the whole of our Western canon. It's Paul's reflection on the nature of mature love. Did he preach these words as well as write them? How did people respond when they heard them?

As beautiful as this passage is though, I often feel despair when I read it. Paul is writing about maturity. I look around at my peers—I'm toward the tail end of the so-called Baby Boomers—and I find myself wondering what our legacy will be, what will we leave behind for our children and our grandchildren? Have we put aside our childish ways? It seems like we've been in a state of perpetual adolescence since the 1960s. I wonder some days if we're really up to doing the hard work of making the world a better place.

It's time to wipe the mirror clean, to look deeply into our faces and really see ourselves—not as we are, but as we can be. As God sees us.

Lord, give me the faith to honestly see what needs to be seen, grant me the hope to heal what needs to be healed, and allow me to experience your gentle love as I put aside my childish ways and answer your call to know fully and to be fully known by you.

The Cross Is the Gospel

Christ did not send me to baptize but to proclaim the gospel, and not with eloquent wisdom, so that the cross of Christ might not be emptied of its power. For the message about the cross is foolishness to those who are perishing, but to us who are being saved it is the power of God.

—1 CORINTHIANS 1:17–18

Paul said many times he preached "Christ crucified." He wants Christians to really understand the Crucifixion before they jump to the triumph of the Resurrection. No matter how wise a person may be—in Paul's time or our own—it's difficult to wrap our minds around the truth of the cross. Paul is suggesting that wisdom and understanding do not suffice where the cross is concerned. Only faith offers us a glimpse of what Paul is proclaiming. There are many ways of seeing and knowing. Faith opens the door to a new way of seeing—as Paul writes, a "more excellent way." It's faith that begins to allow us to experience God's power as a truth that defies all conventional human logic. The suffering that Jesus endured is a mystery we can never truly comprehend and yet Paul teaches that the power of God is found at the foot of the cross.

In the Gospel of Mark, Jesus tells his listeners one of the most perplexing paradoxes of our faith: "If any want to become my followers, let them deny themselves and take up their cross and follow me. For those who want to save their life will lose it, and those who lose their life for my sake, and for the sake of the gospel, will save it." (Mark 8:34–35).

⪢26⪡

Nothing Can
Separate Us from
the Love of God

For I am convinced that neither death, nor life, nor angels, nor
rulers, nor things present, nor things to come, nor powers, nor
height, nor depth, nor anything else in all creation, will be able
to separate us from the love of God in Christ Jesus our Lord.

—ROMANS 8:38–39

My father was a military man, a stoic lifer who seldom complained, certainly not about personal pain. Late on September 10, 2001, I flew to New Mexico from my home in Chicago. I met my two sisters who lived in Albuquerque and we drove all night to Lubbock, Texas, where my father had been taken to the hospital.

We arrived at the Texas Tech University Medical Center early on the morning of September 11. My father's room was crowded with doctors, nurses, and other hospital personnel. Everyone was watching TV, which showed the terrible pictures of the destruction of the World Trade Center.

I learned my father would have exploratory surgery the next day. I also learned that all flights home had been grounded and I would be staying in Lubbock for a few more days. Actually, it turned out to be three weeks.

My father almost died in surgery. The doctors found enough cancer to be uncertain that treatment would be effective. When my father came out of the anesthesia, he looked at me. He didn't say anything, but his steady blue eyes were clear enough. I offered an encouraging smile, and then shook my head slowly from side-to-side. He shrugged and smiled back.

He chose to die at home. My mother gave him wonderful care and support for his remaining days. She was a saint. He died less than four months after leaving the hospital. I wouldn't call my father a religious man, but he believed. As he drew closer to death, I know he spent quiet moments praying with his prayer book from childhood. I wasn't with him when he died but my mother assures me he was serene and peaceful.

I pray he came to know what St. Paul promises each of us in this passage from Romans.

∝27∾

To an Unknown God

Athenians, I see how extremely religious you are in every way, for as I went through the city and looked carefully at the objects of your worship, I found among them an altar with the inscription, "To an unknown god." What therefore you worship as unknown, this I proclaim to you. The God who made the world and everything in it, he who is Lord of heaven and earth, does not live in shrines made by human hands, nor is he served by human hands, as though he needed anything, since he himself gives to all mortals life and breath and all things. . . . For "In him we live and move and have our being"; as even some of your own poets have said, "For we too are his offspring."

—ACTS OF THE APOSTLES, 17:22–25, 28

This passage is the only one I've chosen that is not from Paul's letters, it's from his companion Luke. It is part of Paul's famous speech in the Areopagus, the meeting place of the learned philosophers and teachers of ancient Athens. It is one of the most remarkable Christian homilies ever given, especially considering the name of Jesus is never mentioned.

I suspect that the people who heard this marvelous speech reacted in three distinct ways. First, some simply shook their heads and muttered about not understanding a thing Paul said. A second group was overcome by his message and became ready to drop everything and follow him. A third group was ready to kill him for his arrogance and apparent blasphemy. That's how people usually reacted to Paul. Fortunately, he was usually whisked away by the second group before the third group could get to him.

Here's my version of a familiar story. I see a young Paul, drawing earnestly in the sand. His Greek tutor in Tarsus asks him what he's drawing and Paul says, "I'm drawing God." The tutor pauses and then says, "But Paul, nobody knows what God looks like." Paul stops what he's doing, looks up and says, "When I'm done my work they will."

❦ 28 ❧

The Glory of the Cross

Let the same mind be in you that was in Christ Jesus, who, though he was in the form of God, did not regard equality with God as something to be exploited, but emptied himself, taking the form of a slave, being born in human likeness. And being found in human form, he humbled himself and became obedient to the point of death—even death on a cross.

—PHILIPPIANS 2:5–8

In ancient times the cross was a symbol of fear, shame, and utter defeat. Crucifixion was Rome's way of executing common criminals and anyone else who opposed imperial Roman rule. Imagine wearing a representation of an electric chair around your neck. Imagine a large gallows hanging behind the altar in your church. This is how the cross appeared to the earliest believers.

But not to Paul. For him the cross was a symbol of glory, of the victory of life over death. Paul was one of the first to preach "Christ crucified" and he tried to help his listeners to understand what the sacrifice of Jesus meant. Unlike Adam, a man who aspired to be God, Jesus was God in human form. He suffered the pain of torture, torment, and crucifixion—not as a God, but as a man. As the Eucharistic Prayer says, it was "a death he freely accepted."

What did it mean for Christ to have died on a Roman cross and then come back to life? No wonder Paul preached Christ crucified. The world order had been turned upside down. God had entered human history through the portal of the cross of Jesus. Nothing would be the same. Paul understood this. Paul realized that the ultimate symbol of death and defeat in his world had been reclaimed for the glory of God.

❈ 29 ❈

Do Not Let
the Sun Go Down
on Your Anger

Putting away falsehood, let all of us speak the truth to our neighbors, for we are members of one another. Be angry but do not sin; and do not let the sun go down on your anger.

—Ephesians 4:25–26

In the early twentieth century, the bishop of Paris was a famous evangelizer. He loved to confront cynics, scoffers, and angry unbelievers. He reached out with patience, gentleness, and great love. He was successful in bringing many people to God. He often told this story:

An angry young man would stand outside the Cathedral of Notre Dame in Paris and shout obscenities at people coming and going to church. He would taunt them, insult them, yell derogatory things about their faith, and otherwise cause such a commotion that it was hard to ignore him.

One day, a lowly assistant priest assigned to the cathedral came out to face the angry young man. He said to him, "Let's get this over with once and for all." The young man just cursed at him. So the priest said to the young man, "I dare you to do something that I'm certain you can't do."

"There is nothing you can ask me to do that I can't do if I choose," the young man sneered.

"Well come into the sanctuary with me and stand before the figure of Christ on the cross and shout as loudly as you can three times, 'Christ died on the cross for me and I don't care!'"

The young man went into the sanctuary with the priest, stood before the large crucifix, raised his fist and shouted as loud as he could, "Christ died on the cross for me and I don't care."

"Very good, now do it again" the priest said. The young man shouted again, "Christ died on the cross for me and I don't care." But this time there was a little hitch in his voice.

"Now, say it one more time." The young man raised his fist at the image of Christ on the cross and began to shout but only a strangled cry came out of his mouth and he fell to his knees sobbing.

As he would finish telling this story, the bishop would say, "The defiant young man was me. I was angry and thought I didn't need God. But I was wrong."

∝30∝

Whenever
I Am Weak,
Then I Am Strong

To keep me from being too elated, a thorn was given me in the flesh, a messenger of Satan to torment me, to keep me from being too elated. Three times I appealed to the Lord about this, that it would leave me, but he said to me, "My grace is sufficient for you, for power is made perfect in weakness." So, I will boast all the more gladly of my weaknesses, so that the power of Christ may dwell in me. Therefore I am content with weaknesses, insults, hardships, persecutions, and calamities for the sake of Christ; for whenever I am weak, then I am strong.

—2 CORINTHIANS 12:7–10

Paul suffered enormously. Every time he achieved a measure of success, it was almost always followed by a setback. Still, he plodded on with great tenacity and perseverance. We're not certain what Paul refers to as his "thorn in the flesh." It may have been epilepsy, or asthma, or some other affliction that periodically rendered him unable to travel, speak, or write. Whatever it was, Paul perceives it as from Satan, and accepts that he will have to contend with it. In fact he uses it to more closely identify with the suffering of Christ.

It's hard for me to understand Paul's fierce commitment to his vision in light of the difficulties he faced. Paul was Christ-haunted and we only understand him in the context of his relationship to the risen Christ Jesus. But perhaps to really get Paul, I might have to ask myself a hard question. Can I remain faithful, as Paul did, to the truth I have come to know: that it is in my weakness I find my strength in Jesus?

By Grace You Have Been Saved

By grace you have been saved through faith, and this is not your own doing; it is the gift of God—not the result of works, so that no one may boast. For we are what he has made us, created in Christ Jesus for good works, which God prepared beforehand to be our way of life.

—Ephesians 2:8–10

Consider this passage from Ephesians. If we've been saved by God's merciful grace, and if this gift was prepared for us *before* creation, then we should ask these questions: What have we been saved from and for what purpose? How did God do this before we were even born? What part of me is eternal and connected to God through all time—before this existence and beyond?

Psalm 139:13–18 is a good starting place . . .

> For it was you who formed my inward parts;
>> you knit me together in my mother's womb.
> I praise you, for I am fearfully and wonderfully made.
>> Wonderful are your works;
> that I know very well.
>> My frame was not hidden from you,
> when I was being made in secret,
>> intricately woven in the depths of the earth.
> Your eyes beheld my unformed substance.
> In your book were written
>> all the days that were formed for me,
>> when none of them as yet existed.
> How weighty to me are your thoughts, O God!
>> How vast is the sum of them!
> I try to count them—they are more than the sand;
>> I come to the end—I am still with you.

✑32✑

Think about
These Things

Finally, beloved, whatever is true, whatever is honorable, whatever is just, whatever is pure, whatever is pleasing, whatever is commendable, if there is any excellence and if there is anything worthy of praise, think about these things. Keep on doing the things that you have learned and received and heard and seen in me, and the God of peace will be with you.

—PHILIPPIANS 4:8–9

In my previous work as a literary agent, I would sometimes day-dream about going back in time and signing up writers like Homer, Paul, Luke, Augustine, Dante, and Shakespeare. I'd arrange big book, movie, and television deals for them. The money would come rolling in. What a dream!

Our civilization is built on the great ancient writers and thinkers: Virgil, Seneca, Cicero, and Marcus Aurelius, not to mention Socrates, Plato, and Aristotle, the writers of the Psalms, and whoever wrote Ecclesiastes—"Vanity of vanity, all is vanity," and "For everything there is a season, and a time for every matter under heaven," and don't forget, "there is nothing new under the sun . . ."

Paul is among the greatest of these writers. He has deeply influenced the way we think about God, heaven and the afterlife, church, justice, love, sex, honor, leadership, politics, education, the law, worship, philosophy, and government. But like many giants of the distant past, Paul is more admired than read. Let's *read* him. Let's *learn* from him.

❦33❧

The Wisdom
of This World
Is Foolishness

Do not deceive yourselves. If you think that you are wise in this age, you should become fools so that you may become wise. For the wisdom of this world is foolishness with God.

—1 Corinthians 3:18–19

To the Greeks of Paul's time, the idea that the transcendent God would become involved in the affairs of mortals was nonsense. To the Jews, the notion that Jesus—a condemned, crucified carpenter from Nazareth—could be the son of God was equally baffling.

It seems like an impossible task. How could Paul convince the world that a rural carpenter was the one and only true Son of God, and the path by which God the Father was reconciling the whole broken world to himself?

Obviously Paul had help. Clearly, the Holy Spirit was watching over Paul, helping him perform miracles, assisting him in hair-raising escapes, and inspiring him to write his great letters. Karen Armstrong likened Paul to a journalist writing on napkins and scraps of paper while under fire in war zones, on the run from people trying to kill him. But Paul kept on with his work. He was successful by any measure.

There's a story about Jesus in heaven a few years after the Ascension, someone asks him if he's absolutely sure he left the right people in charge to continue his work and build his kingdom on earth. Jesus looks up, smiles, and says, "I sure hope so, I don't have a backup team."

∝34∝

Let Your Love Be Genuine

Let love be genuine; hate what is evil, hold fast to what is good; love one another with mutual affection; outdo one another in showing honor. Do not lag in zeal, be ardent in spirit, serve the Lord. Rejoice in hope, be patient in suffering, persevere in prayer. Contribute to the needs of the saints; extend hospitality to strangers. Bless those who persecute you; bless and do not curse them. Rejoice with those who rejoice, weep with those who weep. Live in harmony with one another; do not be haughty, but associate with the lowly; do not claim to be wiser than you are. Do not repay anyone evil for evil, but take thought for what is noble in the sight of all. If it is possible, so far as it depends on you, live peaceably with all.

—Romans 12:9–18

Different cultures through the ages have had varied definitions of love. Paul was always sensitive to the nuances of the communities he addressed. For much of the Mediterranean region, love was tied closely to honor, and as such was directed outside oneself. Love was often experienced through the community's appreciation reflected back toward the individual who had done good works.

Today, it seldom feels as if I'm called to be noble, to be honorable—it even sounds quaint, like remnants of the past patriarchy. Men today are celebrated for their more nurturing qualities and I think it's understandable to a degree. But having a noble purpose, striving to be honorable, being inspired by a vision greater than ourselves, being called to serve and steward, to *live in harmony*, this feels right to me as a man. We live in a cynical age and it can render us impotent. I want to live as Paul suggests above. That feels like a challenge worth meeting.

For me, this reading from Romans is one of the great descriptions of what it means to be truly Christian—and also, truly a man.

The Power to Comprehend

I pray that you may have the power to comprehend, with all the saints, what is the breadth and length and height and depth, and to know the love of Christ that surpasses knowledge, so that you may be filled with all the fullness of God.

—Ephesians 3:18–19

I love discovering a piece of writing from an unlikely source and being blown away by it. That happened when I came across a startlingly honest and inspiring piece of spiritual writing from Douglas Coupland, the author of *Generation X.*

In his book, *Life after God*, he writes: "Now—here is my secret: I tell it to you with an openness of heart that I doubt I shall ever achieve again, so I pray that you are in a quiet room as you read these words. My secret is that I need God—that I am sick and can no longer make it alone. I need God to help me give, because I no longer seem capable of giving; to help me to be kind, as I no longer seem capable of kindness; to help me to love, as I seem beyond being able to love."

I don't know much about Coupland but there's almost that desperation for the love of God, or at least the recognition of our deep need for God's love, similar to what courses through all of Paul's writing. "My secret is that I need God—that I am sick and can no longer make it alone."

∝36∞

The Name above
Every Other

*Therefore God also highly exalted him and gave him the name
that is above every name, so that at the name of Jesus every
knee should bend, in heaven and on earth and under the earth,
and every tongue should confess that Jesus Christ is Lord, to
the glory of God the Father.*

—Philippians 2:9–11

The story of Christianity in Europe begins with Paul's arrival in about AD 50 at the city of Philippi in the Roman province of Macedonia in Greece. Philippi lay on the Via Egnatia, the main road between Italy and Byzantium, the two centers of the Roman Empire. Paul arrived in this cosmopolitan Roman colony by ship from Asia Minor on his second missionary journey. He preached, made converts, and set up his first church in Europe in the home of a woman named Lydia. It remained his favorite community of believers. Eventually though, he got into trouble with the local authorities and had to leave town. Luke writes all about it in Acts 16.

Paul does not say where he was imprisoned when he wrote this letter to the church in Philippi, but the fact that he was in prison, that he might be executed, and feared he would never see his friends again, might explain why he wrote with such apparent warmth and affection. But what explains how in those conditions he could write one of the most beautiful and eloquent descriptions of the majesty of Jesus in all of scripture?

◅37▻

The Saints
of Light

May you be made strong with all the strength that comes from his glorious power, and may you be prepared to endure everything with patience, while joyfully giving thanks to the Father, who has enabled you to share in the inheritance of the saints in the light.

—COLOSSIANS 1:11−12

One of my favorite movies is *Chariots of Fire*. It's a story about the British Olympic track team competing in the first games after World War I. Eric Liddell and Harold Abrahams are the main characters. Both are champion runners. Liddell is a devout Christian and won't run on Sundays. Abrahams, a Jew, constantly confronts the prevailing anti-Semitism of the day.

The movie is filled with memorable lines. Harold Abrahams says with exasperation to a friend, "If I can't win, I won't run!" To which she replies, "If you don't run, you can't win." Eric Liddell says at one point in the movie, "I believe God made me for a purpose, but he also made me fast. And when I run I feel his pleasure."

Later, in the face of great pressure, Liddell remains true to his faith by refusing to run a scheduled race on Sunday. He tells the head of the British Olympic delegation and a member of the royal family that, "God made countries, God makes kings, and the rules by which they govern. And those rules say that the Sabbath is his. And I for one intend to keep it that way."

I can imagine Eric Liddell arriving in heaven and Paul waiting for him. Liddell looks at Paul and smiles. Paul smiles back and says, "Eric, you've fought the good fight, you've finished the race, and you kept the faith, welcome."

∞38∞

Aspire to Live Quietly

We urge you, beloved, . . . to aspire to live quietly, to mind your own affairs, and to work with your hands, as we directed you, so that you may behave properly toward outsiders and be dependent on no one.

—1 THESSALONIANS 4:10–12

Ananias is the Christian in Damascus who ministered to Paul immediately after Paul's conversion. Luke tells the story in the ninth chapter of the Acts of the Apostles. Popular stories about Ananias have been told over the centuries, embellished over time, and seasoned with a little myth and a dash of legend. Here's one that inspires me:

Ananias was a simple old man who aspired to live a quiet life. He was a shoemaker of modest means who lived alone in Damascus. He worshipped in the local synagogue and awaited the promised messiah. One day, while praying in the synagogue, he heard an uproar. A group of Jews from out of town was preaching about the Messiah, a Galilean named Jesus who had been killed by the Romans but had risen from the dead. Others were angered by this story. They threw the out-of-towners into the street.

Something about the men caught Ananias's attention; he followed them out into the street where they were laughing.

"Why are you laughing?" Ananias asked. "If I had been thrown out on my head like that I don't know if I would be laughing."

"You would if you knew the Lord," said one of the young men with warmth in his eyes.

"Tell me about this Jesus," Ananias asked. Ananias was baptized and became one of the first disciples in Damascus.

One night, in a dream, the Lord came to him and said, "Ananias, you're a good man, you've led a good life and I have an important task for you."

"Yes, Lord, I'm here, what do you want me to do?"

"Go to a house on Straight Street and there you will find a man named Saul. Tell him about me, heal his blindness, and you will have done a great service."

"But, Lord, isn't he the same man who has been gathering up your followers and throwing them in jail?"

"Yes, but I need him, as I need you. Now go, Ananias."

Ananias went and did as the Lord requested, healed Paul of his blindness, and told him everything he had learned about Jesus. Not long after that, Ananias became ill and died, never knowing what the Lord accomplished through Paul.

So be faithful. Live in peace. Serve the Lord. You never know the good you might do.

❥39❥

A New Creation

If anyone is in Christ, there is a new creation: everything old has passed away; see, everything has become new! All this is from God, who reconciled us to himself through Christ, and has given us the ministry of reconciliation; that is, in Christ God was reconciling the world to himself . . .

—2 CORINTHIANS 5:17–19

Paul's passage above is one of the most important claims he makes about Christ. Everything is new in Christ, and through Jesus, God reconciles all of creation to himself.

I was born blind in my left eye. I still don't understand it when the doctors tell me the cause, but it's irreparable. As a child I was teased because my eye would wander when I was tired. I was self-conscious about it for many years.

When I was nineteen I went to a Benedictine Abbey in the mountains of northern New Mexico to explore the possibility of becoming a monk. While I was there, I asked the abbot, a famous healer, to pray over my eye, and if it was God's will, restore sight to the eye. At first, nothing happened. Then slowly I became aware of light in the eye and gradually I began to see blurry shapes, never in detail, but more than I had before.

I still see very little out of my left eye, but I do have some vision. Sometimes when I pray, I get a sense that my left eye sees to the degree that my faith allows. As my faith grows, perhaps the vision in my left eye will as well. On the other hand, I do believe that someday I will be made new in the Lord and when that day comes I have no doubt I will see the Lord clearly with both eyes.

⤗40⤙

According
to His Mercy

We ourselves were once foolish, disobedient, led astray, slaves to various passions and pleasures, passing our days in malice and envy, despicable, hating one another. But when the goodness and loving kindness of God our Savior appeared, he saved us, not because of any works of righteousness that we had done, but according to his mercy, through the water of rebirth and renewal by the Holy Spirit. This Spirit he poured out on us richly through Jesus Christ our Savior, so that, having been justified by his grace, we might become heirs according to the hope of eternal life.

—TITUS 3:3–7

According to his mercy." In Latin, the word for mercy is *merces,* which means "God's gratuitous compassion." Today we define mercy as the kind or compassionate treatment of an offender, enemy, prisoner, or any other person under one's power.

In Thomas Merton's *The Sign of Jonas,* he has God speak of his "Mercy within mercy within mercy. I have forgiven the universe without end."

In Henri Nouwen's *A Cry for Mercy,* he writes, "God's mercy is greater then our sins."

After his conversion Paul spent his entire life pointing to a new reality: Something profound and life-altering had occurred in the world through Jesus. Despite our history of intolerance, hatred, violence, and every other sin, God had forgiven us—all of us. Through Christ, we've all been renewed, the scales balanced, justice done. There's more: Through Christ, we've even become heirs to the kingdom and the hope of eternal life.

Jesus does all the work, we get the glory. That's God's gratuitous compassion.

⧯41⧯

Justified by Faith

Since we are justified by faith, we have peace with God through our Lord Jesus Christ, through whom we have obtained access to this grace in which we stand; and we boast in our hope of sharing the glory of God . . . but we also boast in our sufferings, knowing that suffering produces endurance, and endurance produces character, and character produces hope, and hope does not disappoint us, because God's love has been poured into our hearts through the Holy Spirit that has been given to us. While we were still weak, at the right time Christ died for the ungodly. Indeed, rarely will anyone die for a righteous person—though perhaps for a good person someone might actually dare to die. But God proves his love for us in that while we still were sinners Christ died for us.

—ROMANS 5:1–8

It's a sad fact that many Christians are bitterly divided over interpretations of this famous passage about the concept of justification (works vs. faith alone). Wars have been fought over such theological differences. Today it's hard to imagine people becoming so inflamed with passion over a theological concept. But then again . . .

Jim Campbell is a friend of mine and a wonderful theologian, writer, and teacher. I asked him to help explain to me what Paul is saying in this selection. Here's my paraphrase of what Jim said:

God alone can justify. God's justice is the highest form of justice. It fulfills, follows, and is greater than the Law; and it honors and keeps all the promises made by God to his covenant people. Only God can reconcile humankind—through the event of Jesus—to himself. We cannot justify ourselves; we cannot win justification; we cannot earn justification in any way. It is only by uniting in faith with Christ Jesus, who won this grace through his sacrifice on the cross, that we are healed and made whole with God and God's creation. This grace is a gift, freely given and freely accepted, and experienced through the actions of the Holy Spirit.

◁42▷

Do This in Remembrance of Me

I received from the Lord what I also handed on to you, that the Lord Jesus on the night when he was betrayed took a loaf of bread, and when he had given thanks, he broke it and said, "This is my body that is for you. Do this in remembrance of me." In the same way he took the cup also, after supper, saying, "This cup is the new covenant in my blood. Do this, as often as you drink it, in remembrance of me." For as often as you eat this bread and drink the cup, you proclaim the Lord's death until he comes.

—1 CORINTHIANS 11:23–26

My work has taken me to many religious communities around the country. I'm usually there to meet a writer who is also a priest. Whenever I can, I stay in the community of the person I'm visiting. I do this to meet people, to share a meal and fellowship, and—most importantly—to worship with them. At Mass—in Texas, New York City, an infirmary chapel in St Louis, or a college campus in Nebraska—I participate in a ritual that hasn't changed much in a long, long time.

At Mass, we all know the prayers, and we all say the words together, we know the appropriate gestures, we move together at the proper times. I become one with their community of worship through this shared expression of faith. It's quite a wonderful gift to a traveling stranger.

Another thing happens later. After Mass, when I see the same people in the hall or in the dining room, it's as if we've already met. We've shared an intimate moment of fellowship. We've discovered that we share a common friend and are awaiting news of his return.

✥43✥

The Good of All

My friends, if anyone is detected in a transgression, you who have received the Spirit should restore such a one in a spirit of gentleness. Take care that you yourselves are not tempted. Bear one another's burdens, and in this way you will fulfill the law of Christ. So let us not grow weary in doing what is right, for we will reap at harvest time, if we do not give up. So then, whenever we have an opportunity, let us work for the good of all, and especially for those of the family of faith.

—GALATIANS 6:1–2, 9–10

From 1966 to 1970 I lived in England. I was eleven when we arrived and had just turned fifteen when we left. I loved England. I loved British culture and the British people. I loved living there and I wept when we returned to the States.

One of our favorite television journalists was Malcolm Muggeridge. Muggeridge was not known as a religious man; in fact I believe at the time he was a professed atheist, who later converted. But he began broadcasting mesmerizing stories about an unusual nun in the streets of Calcutta. His documentary and accompanying book, *Something Beautiful for God* introduced the world to Mother Teresa.

I was intrigued and, truthfully, horrified by the stories of this little nun picking lepers out of the gutters and tending to their wounds, cleaning the maggots out of the running sores of dying street people, finding them food, shelter, and a place to die in peace. I remember asking my mother why anyone would do what Mother Teresa was doing. She said, without missing a beat, "Mother Teresa sees the face of Christ in the poor, the sick, and the dying. Every day that she spends helping the sick and the dying she's mending our broken world by helping her beloved Jesus, who unfortunately we're still rejecting." I said something like, "Right, well thanks, Mom that explains everything."

It's been forty years now and I've seen and experienced a little more suffering. I've lost friends and family members. I see the urban poor and homeless on my way to work every day. I still see a broken world. I think about what my mother said to me all those years ago. I get it now—that does explain everything.

<∞44∞>

What Lies Ahead

Beloved, I do not consider that I have made it my own; but this one thing I do: forgetting what lies behind and straining forward to what lies ahead, I press on toward the goal for the prize of the heavenly call of God in Christ Jesus.

—Philippians 3:13–14

I discovered a hauntingly beautiful song on one of my wife's CDs. It's called "In the Sun." It's been covered by a number of popular musicians but Peter Gabriel's version is the one I'm most familiar with. What first caught my attention were the words *"May God's love be with you . . . always . . ."*

But another line in the song really got me thinking, "If I find my own way, how much will I find. . . ." This line is repeated over and over in the song. After listening to the song hundreds of times I started to think about it in light of what Paul is saying in this passage. If I find my own way, I may not find what I'm looking for. Why? Because the goal isn't me and my way. What I'm looking for is connection, a way to relate to others, a sense of how we all belong together.

We all want to be part of something, a family, a community, something larger than ourselves, larger than our own self-interest— even if we don't specifically know what we're looking for. Paul didn't make it on his own. He doesn't look back but instead strains forward, trusting union with God will be his prize. Paul wanted all of us to finish together, to get where we are going as one.

Mr. Rogers tells a story about a race in the Special Olympics—I think it was the hundred yard dash. One of the participants fell and started crying in frustration. The rest of the runners went back, picked up their fallen comrade, and together, all holding hands, crossed the finish line as one.

∝45∾

The Blood
of His Cross

In him all the fullness of God was pleased to dwell, and through him God was pleased to reconcile to himself all things, whether on earth or in heaven, by making peace through the blood of his cross.

—Colossians 1:19–20

In the ancient world, during the birthing season of sheep, some ewes would give birth to a stillborn lamb and some ewes would die giving birth, leaving orphan lambs. Shepherds would try to put the orphan lamb with the childless ewe, but this didn't work. The ewe could smell that the lamb wasn't her own and would reject it. The lamb would starve to death and the ewe would suffer a mother's broken heart.

To prevent this, shepherds would drain the blood of the dead lamb and bathe the orphan lamb in the blood. The ewe, smelling her own, would allow the lamb to suckle and thereby survive.

We're saying something similar when we refer to Jesus as the Lamb of God. God the Father, through the sacrifice of his only Son, has washed us in Christ's blood, and we are now the Father's own, fully restored, and welcome at his table.

Think about this the next time you hear the words before communion, "This is the Lamb of God, who takes away the sin of the world. Happy are those who are called to his supper."

❧46❧

Be at Peace
among Yourselves

Be at peace among yourselves. And we urge you, beloved, to admonish the idlers, encourage the faint hearted, help the weak, be patient with all of them. See that none of you repays evil for evil, but always seek to do good to one another and to all. Rejoice always, pray without ceasing, give thanks in all circumstances; for this is the will of God in Christ Jesus for you. Do not quench the Spirit. Do not despise the words of prophets, but test everything; hold fast to what is good; abstain from every form of evil. May the God of peace himself sanctify you entirely; and may your spirit and soul and body be kept sound and blameless at the coming of our Lord Jesus Christ.

—1 THESSALONIANS 5:13–23

I think about this story when I read this passage from Paul.

A village had fallen on bad times. For ages it had been a place where neighbors cared for one another and helped each other through difficult times. People were happy and friendly. Travelers loved to visit the village because it was so welcoming. But things inexplicably changed. People began to bicker with one another. They become suspicious of each other. Neighbor stopped talking to neighbor and a dark cloud settled over the village.

The village chief was in despair; he could see things growing worse but didn't know what to do. One day a stranger came to the village. He was a young man, with a confident way about him, and he soon found himself deep in conversation with the chief about the village's problems. The chief said to the stranger, "You seem like an intelligent young man, tell me what you think."

"Well I'm glad you've asked, because that's the reason I'm here. We've just learned the Messiah lives in your village. We're not sure who it is, but we're certain that the Messiah is one of you."

Later that night, the chief shared the young man's puzzling news with his wife. The next day, the chief's wife told her best friend. Within no time, the story spread through the village like wildfire. Then the strangest thing happened. People began to discover the love that they had locked deep in their hearts. They began to treat one another with renewed respect and care. They began to see the goodness in one another again. Slowly, the village was transformed. The chief sent for the young man but he was already gone. He never returned. He didn't have to.

⨯47⨯

The Life That
Really Is Life

Those who in the present age are rich, command them not to be haughty, or to set their hopes on the uncertainty of riches, but rather on God who richly provides us with everything for our enjoyment. They are to do good, to be rich in good works, generous, and ready to share, thus storing up for themselves the treasure of a good foundation for the future, so that they may take hold of the life that really is life.

—1 TIMOTHY 6:17–19

The life that really is life." I wonder what Paul means? I have an idea. I read a wonderful essay called "What Made Paul Tick" written by Jim Manney. Here's part of the essay. It may help you understand the passage above, and help inform your reading of all of Paul's writing.

Paul certainly grasped the implications of the gospel more acutely than anyone else at the time. He saw immediately that the salvation brought by Jesus Christ was a universal, cosmic gift meant for the Gentiles as well as the Jews. He understood that salvation came as a free gift of grace, not as something to be earned by scrupulously observing the law or through any other human work. His life as a missionary was a crusade to announce this good news to as many people as possible.

But Paul's encounter with Christ, and the knowledge he received, do not fully explain his extraordinary transformation. Something deeper than knowledge captured him—and never let go. That something was love. When he met Christ, Paul met overwhelming, all-encompassing, transforming love. He returns again and again to it in his writings. This love propelled his relentless striving.

This is the essential explanation for us as well. Paul knew *about* God's love through his observant Jewish upbringing and the biblical stories of God's dealings with the chosen people. But when he met Jesus in person, he met love itself, and love took over his life.

∝48∞

The Good Fight

As for me, I am already being poured out as a libation, and the time of my departure has come. I have fought the good fight, I have finished the race, I have kept the faith. From now on there is reserved for me the crown of righteousness, which the Lord, the righteous judge, will give me on that day, and not only to me but also to all who have longed for his appearing.

—2 TIMOTHY 4:6–8

I discovered gospel music through Paul. I wanted to hear Paul as well as read him, so I looked for a good spoken version of the New Testament on CD. I bought a set called *Inspired by the Bible Experience.* One of the things the producers have done is break up sections of the readings with gospel music relevant to the passage being read. The song that follows Timothy 4:6–8 references the gospel story of the woman who was hemorrhaging and pursued Jesus for a healing. She was stuck in a crowd. It was hard for her to see Jesus, but she pressed through the crowds and was just able to touch the hem of his garment. Jesus turns and asks who touched him, and when he sees the woman and feels her faith, he heals her.

In the song, recorded live at a worship service, the singers ask God for a healing. Then the minister says that he knows that someone in the congregation needs a healing. He describes the woman in the gospel story, her desperation, her utter fatigue from having been ill for so long, and her belief that only Jesus could heal her if she could just touch him. He challenges his listeners to admit if they've ever been truly desperate like the woman in the story, so desperate they had no one to turn to, nowhere else to go. In that desperation, he asks, would you have the courage to turn to Jesus like she did? Actually, he shouts, "I dare you! I dare you to turn to Jesus."

I was in my car one morning, finishing up some errands, stopped at a red light, listening to that song. I didn't realize my windows were down and shouted back to the minister, "I do, I do turn to you, Jesus!" The people in the car next to me looked over and shook their heads. I held the steering wheel with both hands, stared straight ahead, and said quietly, "I do, I do turn to you, Lord." The light changed and I drove home.

❮49❯

God Is Faithful

God is faithful, and he will not let you be tested beyond your strength, but with the testing he will also provide the way out so that you may be able to endure it.

—1 Corinthians 10:13

Russell Crowe is one of my favorite actors. He's had some of the greatest lines in recent cinema. In *Gladiator*, he plays the good general Maximus. In one scene, before battle with fierce Germanic tribes, he gathers his officers on horseback in a sunlit stand of trees and tells them each to remember that: "What we do in life echoes in eternity." Maximus was a pagan but that's wonderful Pauline theology.

In another movie, *Cinderella Man*, Crowe plays real-life boxer Jim Braddock. When his fortunes take a turn for the worse in the middle of the Great Depression, Braddock refuses to give in or give up. He says to his wife, Mae: "I have to believe that when things are bad I can change them."

Paul was constantly challenged by religious and civil authorities, by imprisonment, by flogging, by stoning, by rejection and betrayal of those closest to him, by shipwrecks and snake bites, by hunger, by thirst, by freezing cold and blistering desert heat. He traveled literally thousands of miles in his lifetime, by foot, by donkey, by cart, by ship, by whatever means necessary. He never gave up.

I watched a miniseries from Italy about the life of Paul; it had some good scenes. I watched another miniseries from 1980 in which Anthony Hopkins captured the passion of Paul. But I'm holding out for Russell Crowe. I want to see him play Paul. I want to see him looking out from a thirty-foot-high movie screen, saying: *"God is faithful, and he will not let you be tested beyond your strength, but with the testing he will also provide the way out so that you may be able to endure it."*

❖ 50 ❖

God Shows
No Partiality

God shows no partiality.

—ROMANS 2:11

Partiality means to choose a piece, a part over the whole, to show preference for one aspect of something over another. This line from the beginning of Paul's letter to the Romans has always jumped out at me. Paul is reminding the small, struggling Christian community in Rome that God does not care if we are "Jew or Greek [Gentile], male or female, slave or free." It doesn't matter to God because it's not about who we are now, or who we were before. It's about who we become in Christ Jesus.

Our culture is obsessed with partiality: we want our children to be gifted and talented, have the best teachers and coaches, and be taught separately from the *average* children; we want them to go to the *best* schools. We prize information that rates the best and worst colleges and the best and worst cities and towns to live in, and the best and worst of everything else from cars and microwave ovens to movies and music. Entire industries do nothing but rate one thing over another. This is useful when we need a new washing machine, but we can never let this mindset extend to how we see people. This is not how God sees his creation.

All of us are invited to the Lord's banquet—the broken and the forgotten along with the best and the brightest. All are called to share in the divine revelation of God's healing love as experienced through the saving grace of Jesus Christ and the Holy Spirit. Paul is making sure we understand that our task as Christians is to be living witnesses to this profound truth.

ᴐ51ᴐ

Above All

As God's chosen ones, holy and beloved, clothe yourselves with compassion, kindness, humility, meekness, and patience. Bear with one another and, if anyone has a complaint against another, forgive each other; just as the Lord has forgiven you, so you also must forgive. Above all, clothe yourselves with love, which binds everything together in perfect harmony. And let the peace of Christ rule in your hearts, to which indeed you were called in the one body. And be thankful. Let the word of Christ dwell in you richly; teach and admonish one another in all wisdom; and with gratitude in your hearts sing psalms, hymns, and spiritual songs to God. And whatever you do, in word or deed, do everything in the name of the Lord Jesus, giving thanks to God the Father through him.

—COLOSSIANS 3:12–17

For those who believe—"God's chosen ones"—our Christian faith is not simply one dimension of who we are; it's an entire way of living, involving the whole community and its well-being.

Paul addressed most of his letters to the growing faith communities he started and to their specific needs and concerns. Christianity, from its earliest days through to our times, has been a struggling communal faith—inwardly directed, but outwardly seeking. The truth of Christ lies in the two greatest commandments: to love one another and to love God. For Paul, all of creation was being healed and restored to God the Father through Christ's redemptive sacrifice on the cross.

When Paul says, *"Above all, clothe yourselves with love,"* he's speaking about love as the highest virtue, which can only be experienced and understood through Jesus. And once we have experienced Jesus on a personal level, Paul is very clear about how we are to conduct our lives: *"And whatever you do, in word or deed, do everything in the name of the Lord Jesus, giving thanks to God the Father through him."*

❁52❁

The Lord Is Near

Let your gentleness be known to everyone. The Lord is near. Do not worry about anything, but in everything by prayer and supplication with thanksgiving let your requests be made known to God. And the peace of God, which surpasses all understanding, will guard your hearts and your minds in Christ Jesus.

—PHILIPPIANS 4:5–7

Scholars say that we've learned more about Paul's world in the last ten or twenty years than we did in the previous two thousand. Paul's life and legacy are being re-examined with great vigor. Pope Benedict XVI has recently declared a Pauline year to honor the great apostle's work. N. T. Wright, one of the leading Pauline scholars of our time, ranks Paul's intellectual contribution to early Western culture as the equivalent of that of Plato, Aristotle, and Seneca. Garry Wills in his best-selling book *What Paul Meant* says that "Paul meant what Jesus meant, that love is the only law." Jerome Murphy-O'Connor writes in his book, *Paul: His Story* that "It's not that the Pauline version of Christianity has failed, it has never been seriously tried." These reappraisals of Paul and his legacy are helping us understand the man and his message more clearly.

I'm not a scholar, but I've learned a lot from Paul after spending nearly every day with him for more than a year. My Paul is certainly the Paul of history, the Paul of the scholars and theologians. But the truth is he's much more to me. I meet my Paul in prayer and reflection. I meet my Paul in the books, songs, paintings, and movies about him. I meet my Paul in those people who are radicalized by his hope-filled spirit of God's love as an instrument of positive and peaceful social change. I meet my Paul in the legacy of a message that revolutionized the ancient world and a message no less meaningful for the modern world.

But more than any other place, I meet my Paul in the pages of the Bible, through his words: *"The Lord is near. Do not worry about anything . . . and the peace of God, which surpasses all understanding, will guard your hearts and your minds in Christ Jesus."*

Epilogue:
If God Is for Us

If God is for us, who is against us? He who did not withhold his own Son, but gave him up for all of us, will he not with him also give us everything else?

—Romans 8:31–32

I've sat with this passage too long now and it's time to end this small book, even though this book is part of a larger journey that will never really end for me. If I'm honest with myself, I could probably spend the rest of my life contemplating this one passage from St. Paul. The magnitude of what Paul says is overwhelming. The realization of what God offers is staggering. So what's the next step? For me, it's simple. If God withholds nothing from me, I choose not to withhold anything from God. If God offers "everything else" including Jesus, I choose to match that offer as best I can. I offer my life, my dreams, my hopes, my fears, my will, my work, and my time. I offer my family: my wife and my children. I offer my friends. I offer my enemies, whoever they may be. I offer the homeless woman on the bridge by the train station. I offer a world that is too complex for me to understand most days but not so big that God can't heal it and bring it into harmony. I offer this present moment, now, and the unfolding now that becomes the next moment and the next tomorrow.

And as I look down the road of my tomorrows, I can just make out a hunched-over man with a walking stick in hand, ragged robe, bowlegged, strands of unruly hair, an alarming beard, and eyes that are hard to look away from. He's waving me over and he's inviting me to walk with him for awhile. There's something about his face that's so welcoming. When I ask where we're going he assures me that the journey is our destination and we pray this one with our feet. He has that quality about him, you trust him. He smiles patiently, it's my call, and I realize that wherever he's headed, I'd be honored to travel there with him. And so we begin walking . . .

Scripture Citations

Acknowledgments

This book became possible because of the good people at Loyola Press who supported the idea, gave me the tools and the time for writing, and offered patient advice and constant inspiration throughout. Special thanks to George Lane, SJ, Paul Campbell, SJ, and Terry Locke.

Also my deepest gratitude to Jim Campbell, Vinita Wright, Melissa Tomar, Michelle Halm, Judine O'Shea, and Sharon Roth—colleagues and professionals who all made contributions to help this small book be the best it could be. Finally, to Matthew Diener, who brings his best game with him every day—thanks for all your patient help.

Annotated Companion Resources

Most journeys benefit from good traveling companions—friends who can share the best of the discoveries we make along the way, and guides who help us through the most difficult crossings. I was very fortunate in my Pauline journey. Over the year I spent working on the book I had many powerful conversations with Tom McGrath, who shares a tremendous enthusiasm for St. Paul in his own life. His deep listening and encouragement for my journey blessed every step I made. Jim Manney helped me through some of the more profound moments, times when I caught a glimpse of who Paul really is and what he means to each of us, and more importantly, who he's always pointing us toward. I especially want to thank Jim for the phone calls when something Paul had written reduced me to inarticulate weeping. You were so supportive and patient. I still can't get through Romans 8:38–39 without crying. And finally, my good friend Bret Nicholaus, who from day one, when I described this idea, was supportive and provided constant and welcome critique. Our conversations on the "L" during our long commutes home helped me more than you know and your witness helps me to see Paul every day in our world. Ultimately, what I've written is a small book. But there's nothing small about the contribution of the companions who have made my journey possible.

Now for some of the nonhuman companions I found along the way. I used many resources to get a greater understanding of St. Paul's life, his message, and his world, but these are the highpoints—the books, CDs, DVDs that made the journey richer by far.

NONFICTION

Brauch, Manfred T. *Hard Sayings of Paul.* InterVarsity Press: Downers Grove, IL, 1989.

> *Any study of St. Paul will inevitably raise as many questions as it will answer. This book will help you gain a perspective on some of the more challenging statements St. Paul made.*

Dunn, James D. G. *The Cambridge Companion to St. Paul.* Cambridge University Press: Cambridge, UK, 2003.

> *This volume features chapters written by many of the leading Pauline scholars of our time and is organized in a particularly helpful way.*

Griffith-Jones, Robin. *The Gospel According to Paul: The Creative Genius Who Brought Jesus to the World.* HarperSanFrancisco: San Francisco, CA, 2004.

> *This is a rollicking, entertaining, oversized look at St. Paul. I really loved the author's energy and passion. This is a highly rewarding book and a great starting place for learning about St. Paul.*

Harrington, Daniel J. *Paul's Prison Letters: Spiritual Commentaries on Paul's Letters to Philemon, the Philippians, and the Colossians.* New City Press: Hyde Park, NY, 1997.

> *Harrington, a Jesuit priest, writes about St. Paul with authority and concision. His commentary on the prison letters will not only add greater context and understanding of your knowledge of St. Paul, but also open your heart to a deeper spiritual experience of the great apostle.*

Murphy-O'Connor, Jerome. *Paul: His Story*. Oxford University Press: Oxford, UK, 2004.
A wonderful, inspiring look at the life of St. Paul; highly recommended.

Sanders, E. P. *Paul: A Very Short Introduction*. Oxford University Press: Oxford, UK, 2001.
This is part of a great series of brief, often brilliant books by leading scholars on their topics of expertise. Sanders is among the most influential of our contemporary Pauline experts, and this little book is terrific.

Soards, Marion L. *The Apostle Paul: An Introduction to His Writings and Teaching*. Paulist Press: New York, NY, 1987.
An accessible textbook that serves as a solid introduction to the life, letters, and theology of St. Paul.

Wills, Garry *What Paul Meant*. Viking: New York, NY, 2006.
I love this book. The author's insights into St. Paul are remarkable. This highly recommended work is small, but potent.

Witherington, Ben, III. *The Paul Quest: The Renewed Search for the Jew of Tarsus*. InterVarsity Press: Downers Grove, IL, 1998.
The last three decades have brought immense new developments in understanding St. Paul and his world. This book offers a highly readable survey of those developments by a biblical scholar who writes successfully for a popular readership.

Wright, N. T. *What Saint Paul Really Said: Was Paul of Tarsus the Real Founder of Christianity?* W. B. Eerdmans Publishing Co.: Grand Rapids, MI, 1997.

Wright, N. T. *Paul: In Fresh Perspective*. Fortress Press: Minneapolis, MN, 2006.
Wright is perhaps the foremost Pauline scholar of the day and one of the leading contributors to the emerging and sometimes

controversial *"new perspectives"* on Paul and his world. He is an engaging writer and generous thinker, often as charming as he is knowledgeable.

FICTION

Cannon, James. *Apostle Paul: A Novel of the Man Who Brought Christianity to the Western World.* Steerforth: Hanover, NH, 2005.

A wonderful, though underappreciated, narrative fictional account of the life of St. Paul. I found this a captivating read, and the author is to be commended for his stunning re-creation of the world of St. Paul.

Coupland, Douglas. *Life after God.* Pocket Books: New York, NY, 1994.

Special thanks to Douglas Coupland, whose book has nothing whatsoever to do with St. Paul but was definitely inspiration for my book on St. Paul. It was in this book I encountered one of the clearest modern statements of a St. Paul-like hunger for God— just stunning and brave.

Wangerin, Walter. *Paul: A Novel.* Zondervan Publishing House: Grand Rapids, MI, 2000.

Impressionistic, poetic, multivoiced novel on the life of St. Paul, the book starts a little slow but soon picks up speed and delivers a powerfully emotional ending.

STORY COLLECTIONS

Bausch, William J. *A World of Stories for Preachers and Teachers: And All Who Love Stories That Move and Challenge.* Twenty-Third Publications: Mystic, CT, 1998.

Cavanaugh, Brian. *The Sower's Seeds: 120 Inspiring Stories for Preaching, Teaching, and Public Speaking.* Paulist Press: Mahwah, NJ, 2004.

Silf, Margaret. *One Hundred Wisdom Stories from Around the World.* Pilgrim Press: Cleveland, OH, 2003.

White, William R. *Stories for the Journey: A Sourcebook for Christian Storytellers.* Augsburg Publishing House: Minneapolis, MN, 1988.

Videos

Paul the Apostle from *The Bible Collection*, directed by Roger Young, 180 minutes, 2004.

This German/Italian TV miniseries has an unnecessary bad-guy subplot and some hammy moments. But it also features several scenes from the life of St. Paul that are beautifully filmed and undeniably moving.

Peter and Paul, directed by Robert Day , 194 minutes, 1981.

This epic 1981 miniseries features a fiery performance by Anthony Hopkins as St. Paul. I felt this film caught much of heartbreak St. Paul encountered and ultimately overcame.

The Story of Paul the Apostle, from *The Apostles Collection*, 66 minutes, 2003.

Solid documentary done for the History Channel.

Empires: Peter & Paul and the Christian Revolution, 110 minutes, 2003.

Very well-produced PBS documentary on the beginnings of Christianity and its two most important apostles.

The Search for Paul, 88 minutes, ABC News Presents, Peter Jennings Reporting, 2004.

Peter Jennings is terrific in this documentary filmed in the footsteps of St. Paul. He also interviews many of the leading Pauline scholars. This is highly recommended.

Audio Cd

Inspired by . . . the Bible Experience: The New Testament, 18 CDs and 1 "making of" DVD, Zondervan, 2007.

When I desired to hear St. Paul's words brought to life with passion and poetry I was blessed to discover this extraordinary audio production, featuring Today's New International Version of the Bible and the vocal talents of some of my favorite actors including Cuba Gooding Jr., Samuel L. Jackson, and Denzel Washington. This CD set also contains a number of devotional songs performed by top gospel choirs that create the feel of sitting in a joy-filled, African-American church on fire with the Holy Spirit.

Internet

The Paul Page http://www.thepaulpage.com/ is a great resource for keeping up on articles, papers, reviews, and announcements about Pauline studies.